AUSTRALIAN POETRY
1969

AUSTRALIAN POETRY

1969

Selected by
VIVIAN SMITH

ANGUS AND ROBERTSON

First published in 1969 by
ANGUS & ROBERTSON LTD

221 George Street, Sydney
54 Bartholomew Close, London
107 Elizabeth Street, Melbourne
65 High Street, Singapore

© *Angus & Robertson Ltd 1969*

National Library of Australia
REGISTRY NUMBER AUS 69-2010

SBN 207 95219 1

*Published with the assistance of the
Commonwealth Literary Fund*

*Registered in Australia for
transmission by post as a book*

PRINTED IN AUSTRALIA BY
HALSTEAD PRESS, SYDNEY

ACKNOWLEDGMENTS

To the *Age* for "Home-coming" by Bruce Dawe, "Heaven, in a Way" by Rodney Hall, and "Hanover Street" by Andrew Taylor; the *Australian* for "Flying Fox" by Thomas W. Shapcott, "Diver" by R. A. Simpson, "Signs" by Chris Wallace-Crabbe, and "Two Sides of a Story" by Judith Wright; the *Bulletin* for "Snowbound" by Alexander Craig, and "Two Poems" by Elizabeth Riddell; the *Listener* for "Seahorses" and "The History of Music" by Peter Porter; the *London Magazine* for "The Sadness of the Creatures" by Peter Porter; *Meanjin* for "Fifth Anniversary" by Laurence Collinson, "Sorting Papers" and "Invocation of Josefa Asasela" by R. D. FitzGerald, "After Many Campaigns, the Reunion" by Noel Macainsh, "Cave" by Roland Robinson, and "Balmoral, Summer" by Vivian Smith; *Poetry: Australia* for "The Wanderer" by Bruce Beaver, and "Dust to Dust" by Gwen Harwood; *Poetry Magazine* for "Elegy" and "Memories of a Veteran" by Douglas Stewart, and "Wallace Stevens" by Peter Skrzynecki; *Quadrant* for "Winter Matins" by R. F. Brissenden, "Father and Child" by Gwen Harwood, "A Visit to the Ruins" by A. D. Hope, "The Globe" by Margaret Irvin, "I. M. Kenneth Mackenzie" by Evan Jones, "In the Huon Valley" by James McAuley, "The Marriage: beccaficos" by Grace Perry, and "Allies of Nature" by Chris Wallace-Crabbe; *Solidarity* for "The Dead Astronaut" by Judith Wright; *Southerly* for "The Chair" by Douglas Stewart; the *Sydney Morning Herald* for "A Walk in the Park" by Rosemary Dobson, "Sittings by Appointment Only" by Bruce Beaver, "Leviathan" by John Blight, "A Man Talks to Himself" by J. M. Couper, "The Place" and "Easy Does

Acknowledgments

It" by Bruce Dawe, "Continuum" by Eric Irvin, "Snapshots for Margot" by Evan Jones, "The Telescope at Siding Spring" by Geoffrey Lehmann, "Once in a Lifetime, Snow" by Les A. Murray, "Scene: Alexandra Tea Room" by Hal Porter, "Family Happiness" by J. R. Rowland, and "Hell" by Chris Wallace-Crabbe; *Westerly* for "The Widow" by Joan Mas; Angus & Robertson Ltd for poems from *Selected Poems* by David Campbell, *New Poems 1965-69* by A. D. Hope, and *A Counterfeit Silence* by Randolph Stow; South Head Press for poems by Craig Powell and Bruce Beaver; *XI Hunter Valley Poets + VII*, for "Listening to T'ang Poetry", by Norman Talbot.

CONTENTS

Contents

Contents

Contents

INVOCATION OF JOSEFA ASASELA

Robert D. FitzGerald

Much I have had in mind,
lately, a lonely man,
not of my race or kind,
dying far from his own;
who, in a fickle shift
of Arctic wind, was lost
on pack-ice driven adrift—
reft from his frozen coast;

and have considered much,
bewildered—and with distress
for all caught in the clutch
of the claws of loneliness—
whether this man who sought,
strangely, to live apart,
lived with a mastering thought
or was distraught in his heart.

Certainly there have been
lovers of solitude:
some who have found therein
strength, or a faith renewed,
and so have turned from the street,
the till, the desk or the sword,
not in the hour of defeat
though in retreat from the horde—

men for whom, because
of rich companionships
in books or thoughts, it was
good to achieve eclipse,

and who—after riding the surge
of public affairs—would save
integrity; lest it merge
in the turgid wake of the wave.

But here was a village lad
under a tropic day,
born to its life, and bred
to the old, shared, island way
of laughter and work that blend
with custom and death and birth—
what did he think to find
at the utter end of the earth?

Kandavu men, it is said,
have backs that will only stretch
on a foreign mat for a bed,
and legs with a nagging twitch;
and you'll find Kandavu-born
in trading-craft that ride
from Cancer to Capricorn,
on every turn of the tide.

A digging-stick is the tool
to toughen hands of the young;
and the reef grows fish. A fool
believes a traveller's tongue.
Distance, where it unfurls,
drops hunger; it spills no balms
on the weary, like feasts or girls. . . .
But the sea-wind swirls through the palms.

And Asasela was one
who, much like all the rest,
found communal discipline
little turned to his taste.
So it was up and go
to ships and the world's girth,
desertion in Mexico,
then slow months working north.

Authorities missed or lost
the intruder; for he went
beyond two frontiers (crossed
by stealth or by accident)
and on unhindered, except
as dazed by crowds in a town;
ate if he could; and slept
where he stumbled, dropped, lay down.

So, struggling still, he found
the place and the years that were
to become his life, his mind,
as trapper and craftsman in fur,
skilled at fashioning a glove
or handling dogs in the snow
of the climate he came to love
above the warm long-ago.

Half a life back I heard
of the man's cold death; though then
his name was only a word
and a wonder, forgotten again—

nothing one could attach
to scenes that memory views;
just what an eye might catch
in a corner patch of the news.

But now, impelled by a trick
of conscience, I invoke
this man who turned his back
on his age, his home, his folk—
partly a matter of pride
in the body's powers—and I ask:
Were the calls of his day denied?
Did he step aside from a task?

Yet with this thought like a thorn
in my own skin, I can
still somewhat try to discern
qualities in the man
not wholly cause for reproof
if one had rods to probe
a mind in-turned and aloof
on the ice-clad roof of the globe.

For in space-like loneliness
there can be silence, deep
as the soul's own silences;
nor is it merely escape
to choose to be one with the work
of storm and stars, although
as a life no more than a spark
in the polar dark and the snow.

Asasela I read
as man the seeker, caught
less in the complex need
of the mind to grow into thought
than in the primal appeals
of challenge and daring choice,
like the hunt for the finer seals
far out on the miles of ice.

In his tent on the shore were found
his diary, his bible, his traps.
Beyond in the opening sound
was the running ice in the rips.
And, low in the sky, the sun
in its unsetting path
may have seemed, like a sign, to atone
for the loneliness of his death.

SORTING PAPERS

Robert D. FitzGerald

Living this while has meant one was immersed
so deep within that process that much has gone
which by mere looking-on
some trifler might have relished from the first

and so preserved like a time-treasured book
spread on the knee through fireside evenings—
unforgettable things
given the mind by just that passing look.

Tussle was well; but now one should discard
old aims like worn possessions, once of worth.
One cannot own the earth;
therefore I burn these papers in my yard

wishing I could sort values out so soon
and choose and bind the handful to be kept,
then afterwards accept
what medicine or sugar is in the spoon,

and be no longer ashamed to let drift by
this bait or that which on a tensing of will
were within reach of skill
jealous, or boastful under a neighbour's eye.

—

TWO POEMS

Elizabeth Riddell

I. TOGETHER

The autumn night moves on your listening face.
I think you wait for me to give you news
Of a half-recollected, half-imagined place
We shared. But was summer country
Tossed with birds and lemon groves.
The pastures shimmered in a coloured dream.
Sunsets like wounds bled on our mutual sky.

What if I tell you all the signs are down,
The tracks grassed over, the maps destroyed and I
No longer speak the language?

From silence we came together and now return
To silence again, each in his lonely skin.

II. ALONE

Locked in this cell of flesh, I am alone.
I listen to the slow creep of my blood
Along the veins, the chime of bone with bone,
Air like a sibilance, whispering in the lung.
My eyes are quiet in their lake of tears.
Prisoner and gaoler in the same cell,
I catch my breath
For sounds of love or death,
Only the pulse responds
To say that all's not done.

A VISIT TO THE RUINS

A. D. Hope

This charming archaeologist, with her spade,
Surveys my ruins, measures the daisied mound,
Three mouldering plinths, one column still erect.
Her twenty summers from its millennial shade
Take stock of all that history underground.
Cutting the first sods, what does she expect?

Has she some theory, or is she digging blind?
Does dream or sober fact impel her, while
She sinks a trial trench, pegs out her grid?
Is it foreknowledge of what she hopes to find
Moulds her young mouth to that archaic smile?
And when her spade rings on the marble lid,

The King's sarcophagus, all its seals intact,
Still smiling will she raise his golden mask,
Touch with warm lips that face of crumbling
        bone,
Or will its hollow sockets not refract
Tears dropping from live eyes again? I ask,
Will she disturb my quiet or her own?

Or, if she seeks inscriptions, to restore
From primitive script my long lost Song of
        Songs,
Whose extant fragments baffle her scholar's art,
Has she the scholar's instinct, which before
She spells its words, by the true Gift of Tongues,
Can call their music already from her heart?

Thinking to reconstruct me as I was
In the great years before the Kingdom fell,
Can she imagine such arrogant splendour; can
Her notes from cinder, debris, sherds and dross
Bring to fierce life the tale these relics tell
Of those last moments when the sack began:

The throne-room wrecked, the roar of "kill and
    kill!"
The women raped and slaughtered where they
    lie,
The shattered images ravished of their gold,
And, whiter than his statue and as still
The young King, dying in all that butchery,
Watching the hangings as the flames take hold?

Well if she can! Some things her practised eye
Will miss: her sceptic mind will not observe
Ghosts slink to deeper layers among the dead;
She will not hear a skeleton's minimal sigh
Greet the sharp sun, nor, as she turns fresh turf,
The mandrake's shriek, torn bleeding from its bed.

No training could enable her to foresee
Her last discovery when it comes to pass:
The eponymous founder's tomb, identified.
Gapes as the granite slab is levered free;
She steps towards that black hole and sees, alas,
That there is nothing, nothing at all inside!

Nothing . . . and then the darkness swirls and
    sighs
And, out of the illimitable past,

A. D. Hope

A voice of terror, speaking her own tongue,
Calls her by name, and calls again, and cries:
"At last you have come home, at last, at last!
Where have you been, child, why did you stay
    so long?"

CROESUS AND LAIS

A. D. Hope

Breakfasting after a romp in the hay,
"Tell me, Lais," said Croesus one day,
"Tell me: this palace, this vast estate,
These hangings, these ivories, jewels and plate,
The bank in the city, the mines in Spain,
Your flocks and forests, your fields of grain;
For wealth like this I have toiled and sweat,
Denied myself pleasure and sleep to get,
And now that I have them, am ready to die
And yet you are almost as rich as I,
And lively and blooming and young as well.
How do you manage it, Lais, tell?"

"The answer is easy, my friend," she said:
"All of these treasures were earned in bed.
You for your riches must cheat or subdue
Men just as cunning and greedy as you;
For every sixpence you win, no doubt
There is somebody else who must do without;
But I grow rich by loving and giving,
Grace, good humour and cheerful living;
And those who are able come here to buy
What to most mortals the gods deny.
It may cost a fortune to sleep with me,
But I give good value, you must agree."

"Don't think me rude," said Croesus and smiled,
"But that is the point in question, child:
A night in your arms, no man denies,
Is the nearest he borders on Paradise;

A. D. Hope

But a night is a night and is quickly past
And things of value are things that last.
This talent of gold I lay at your feet
Might buy me a palace or furnish my fleet—
Not that I grudge it, you understand,
But value is always a bird in the hand:
Love is a bird in the bush, they say,
And what is there left when he flies away?"

"Croesus, my dear, you may think it absurd,
But for one song of that exquisite bird,
Men much wiser and richer than you
Have ventured their lives and their fortunes too.
And since, as you say, you are growing old,
Which would you rather: my body to hold
One short night, or this gold to save
A thousand years in the thankless grave?
And now you must take your leave, I fear:
Lycos my poet will soon be here,
And the rule of this house, as you know, my
        sweet,
Is that my lovers never shall meet."

"Lycos!" cried Croesus, "I think it hard
To pack me off for that beggarly bard,
Drunkard and scandalous rake as well;
What can you see in him, Lais, tell?
But sure, you are teasing to hear me scold:
How would *he* come by a talent of gold?"
"The answer is easy, Croesus, my friend:
He shall have your talent to save or spend.
Beggar and wastrel he well may be,

But the Muses have blessed him as Venus me.
For a night in his arms and a song from his lips
My beauty shall outlast the world's eclipse
And live in his verse, for the pleasure it gave
A thousand years of the thankless grave."

PARADISE SAVED

(another version of the Fall)

A. D. Hope

Adam, indignant, would not eat with Eve,
They say, and she was driven from his side.
Watching the gates close on her tears, his pride
Upheld him, though he could not help but grieve

And climbed the wall, because his loneliness
Pined for her lonely figure in the dust:
Lo, there were two! God who is more than just
Sent her a helpmeet in that wilderness.

Day after day he watched them in the waste
Grow old, breaking the harsh unfriendly ground,
Bearing their children, till at last they died;
While Adam, whose fellow God had not replaced,
Lived on immortal, young, with virtue crowned,
Sterile and impotent and justified.

TREE POEM

W. Hart-Smith

   a tree
is a plain of in
finite finite dim
   ension
      cut into
a hundred
hundred thousand
pieces all reassembled
      to occupy a minimum
   of space
   overlapping
   without over
   lapping

   a tree
is the surface
of a lake of infinite fin
ite extension a
      surface
   sprayed with a poly
   thene film
   and cut into pieces all
rearranged
   to occupy the
   smallest possible three
   dimensional space
      consistent
      with
      most
      efficient
      transpiration

W. Hart-Smith

a tree
is a factory manufacturing
long polymer molecules
with a
tall
chimney
spewing forth
the breath
of life
as a waste product

LEVIATHAN

John Blight

What sort of Age has come never to see again
a whale along our beach. For inshore basking,
    when
I was a trusting youth, a lonely child of ten,
I understood the truth of seeing the great whales.
Now, who'd believe if ten, and not deny such
    tales,
talk of leviathan. Imagination fails
the measurements of them. Tails seen against the
    sky,
when I was young, flung high, higher than the
    eye
could see not opening wide; and even their young
    fry
larger than a bull. The sea was full of them,
whales for everyday, each whale a vital poem
impressed upon the mind. And, mindful now of
    them,
I ask—who killed the whales? That fiercest
    monster, man.
Now no child understands what we all saw when
    ten.

ELEGY

Douglas Stewart

Oh I see clearly since cats and crocodiles and mice
Will never stop breeding because it is natural and
    nice
We must submit to death however it may hurt
Because it was half of the bargain from the start.

I do submit then, I acknowledge death is sensible,
Only it bites me and I feel it reprehensible;
The world is too crowded and death does trim it
    neatly
But I have been too much surrounded by it lately.

I mourn for my black-furred she-cat, and my
    father and my mother
And my aunt and my fierce proud uncle, if there
    isn't any other
Just now to lament, I dread what may lie in store
And I pray that death won't occur on the earth
    any more.

Take Mrs Tiddles now. Tiddles was my cat
And a mother of sixty kittens in five years flat;
But a kind cat, Tiddles, a soft cat, knew her
    station,
And was killed today by a bloody great Alsatian.

Take Eileen FitzGerald now, she was my aunt,
About the size of a peanut, whom nothing could
    daunt;
At the age of eighty wanted to fly a helicopter
And would have, too, only a heart attack stopped
    her.

Take Gerald FitzGerald who fought in the first
    world war
Where the black trenches cut across France like
    a scar
And, wounded somewhere, never stopped fighting
    after
But shook sometimes with a witty, bitter laughter.

Take, since he's taken indeed, Alec Stewart my
    father
Whom we dropped in his grave beside the blue
    sea water.
There in his green hill, far far away he lies
And stares through the earth at the sea with his
    big brown eyes.

Take Mary Stewart, who was Mary FitzGerald
    my mother,
And lie on her gently cold Eltham earth and
    weather;
So young she went, and so much gaiety in her—
But I'll not speak when grief's too deep to utter.

Oh they all live, perhaps, cats, parents and aunt,
Somewhere in shining heaven, but maybe they
    don't;
The cat is her kittens, and only poor souls in me
My father walks and my mother's blue eyes see.

I weep for what is no more, the strong personality,
The person walking the world in all its vitality;
I mourn for those who mean nothing to anybody
But once were the pillars of the earth and held
    me so steady.

Douglas Stewart

True, I have seen old bones like a stone or a daisy
Cows' bones, sheep's bones, lying in the sun so
    easy,
And men's bones too, and I know that old death
    is nothing,
It is only the immediate that hurts, when the live
    thing stops breathing.

But these stood so close to me once and these are
    so recent,
My cat and my aunt are gone, and it is not decent.
I had not thought they were crowding the earth
    so thickly.
Oh earth, oh sun, oh rain, clean their bones
    quickly,

So once again but not with so much hurt
I may admit what I know for the truth in my
    heart,
Life was the half we had and the fine lovely part
But death was the rest of the bargain right from
    the start.

THE CHAIR

Douglas Stewart

I knew a man so old he was like an angel,
Light so consumed him he glittered as frail as
    crystal;

And as he lay on his pillow in his white hair
He fixed his blue eyes on an object, and it was a
    chair.

But was it a chair? It was so strange a shape
He thought he had dragged it over the edge of
    sleep.

It seemed to waver, it was all hollows and space,
It was hardly there, and yet beyond doubt it was.

See it had legs, one two, yes, three and four,
Rounded and tapered, so delicately set on the floor;

And round the legs ran a rung in a pretty ring
He touched it in thought like a harper touching
    a string.

Oh it was a chair all right, there was the seat
In its dainty circle, waiting for someone to sit;

How perfectly shaped it was for sitting upon,
Like a saddle on a little horse, but the horse was
    gone.

And when he thought of all who had sat in that
    chair,
The beautiful ladies, the children floating in air,

And elephants hauling its timber in misty greenery
And sawmills ringing with their singing keen
    machinery,

And the chairs before it, right back to when
    chairs began
Far in dim time past Sheraton and Queen Anne,

That lovely procession of chairs, with people
    sitting
Or about to sit, and smiling and fading and
    flitting,

How wonderful it was to lie in the universe
Where of all lucky things men had made chairs.

To look at a chair and see it look back at him
    squarely—
Oh why had he never observed a chair so clearly?

He must own a hundred himself, at any rate fifty,
Kitchen and dining and drawing room, one for
    the baby—

When he got home he would touch them one by
    one,
He would notice each chair before he dared to
    sit down;

He wished he had noticed them before, but here
    they all were
Melting together, merged in this single chair.

It seemed to move, but did it? No, it stayed put,
So lightly touching the floor with each exquisite
    foot.

What craftsman had made it for him with plane
and with chisel
And built it so fine that now it was floating a
little

So that alone in space it had its strange being
Down that long tunnel of light at the end of his
seeing—

Oh high in that crystal dazzle shining it stood
Carved upon space, that queer sweet shape of
wood,

Far and so clear. . . . I had another old friend
Who said to me once when he knew he was near
his end,

"I am not afraid of death, but how will it come?"
And I could have said but embarrassment struck
me dumb:

"I knew a man who died without fear or care
In absolute ecstacy, thinking about a chair."

MEMORIES OF A VETERAN

Douglas Stewart

Here comes an old soldier from World War One,
He fought not at Ypres, he was far from Verdun,
But he won the last battle (oh do break it down).

Then spare him a copper or buy him a beer
For he fought a lone fight (break it down) with-
     out fear
And when the war started his age was one year.

Three uncles I had, their name was FitzGerald,
They sailed off for France with their lives sore
     imperilled
To fight with the Kaiser with whom they had
     quarrelled.

Good luck to you then, Roy, Gerald, and Maurice,
Away where the nations were fighting like furies,
No doubt you did well but I've my own stories.

I recall (break it down) when I was a boy
Who played with a popgun and thought it a toy
The Germans took prisoner my bold uncle Roy.

But the war was far off from fair Eltham, New
     Zealand,
So I played by the creek with my friend Seymour
     Haden
And little we dreamed what the future kept
     hidden.

And Roy had a mind to fight on for his country,
He tunnelled for miles and when checked by a
sentry
He calmly rode out in a truck-load of laundry.

On charged the brave British, the Germans were
reeling,
At last it was won and the church bells were
pealing
And great was the joy then in Eltham, New
Zealand.

The Town Band was playing, the Kilties were
swinging,
The fire-bell as well as the church bells were
ringing,
The whistles were blowing, men shouting and
singing;

The Kaiser, alas just a dummy of course,
Was dragged through the town in Sam Pepperill's
hearse,
The *Argus* was filled with bad prose and worse
verse,

Such banners, such cheering, such blowing of
bugles,
And up to the Park now the crowd seethes and
struggles
And proudly amongst them march Seymour and
Douglas.

Douglas Stewart

And high on a plank in the Park stood the
   Mayor,
And the local M.P., and the parsons were there
All up on the platform world peace to declare.

Here comes an old soldier, I said so before,
And mine be the first drop of ale that you pour
For I won the last fight in the war to end war.

For young Seymour in spite or some awful mishap
(Break it down, break it down, there's no chance
   of escape)
Knocked off and tramped on my field-marshal's
   cap.

At Eltham on Peace Day began this great fight,
For Douglas hit Seymour, it seemed only right,
And Seymour hit Doug on the nose where it
   hurt.

And away from the Mayor in the midst of his
   speech
The people came rushing like waves on the beach,
They formed in a ring and they roared at each
   punch.

And Douglas hit Seymour and Seymour hit
   Douggie
On the nose (break it down), on the ribs, in the
   belly,
Till Seymour was winded and Douglas was
   groggy.

Oh I fear that our heroes weren't fitted for war,
They met not in rapture in battle's first jar
But circled each other in fear from afar,

But the crowd hemmed them in with its roars and
    its cheers,
They had to fight on, it seemed for four years,
Till Seymour was bleeding and Doug was in tears.

So here's an old soldier and long may he thrive,
He fought a great fight and he came back alive
To be cheered by all Eltham, a victor, aged five.

He's not one to fight now, he's not one to quarrel,
So spare him a copper and tip up the barrel,
And at least (break it down) he'll not point you
    the moral.

OFFICE BLOCK

John Manifold

The main construction is in flexibrick,
Pre-stressed, fatigue-proof, never used before;
It's only fifteen millimetres thick
But carries eighteen thousand tons and more.

The lifts are—damn it, this one seems to stick—
The lifts are atom-driven—mind the door!—
With cybernetic halts. They're pretty slick.
Now, up we go again. Excelsior!

The helicopter-park is just behind
With robots in attendance. But it's queer,
You'd never dream how hard it's been to find
The class of tenant we expected here.

There have been applicants; but now and then
I've had suspicions they were only men.

CONTINUUM

Eric Irvin

Lost melodies sound echoes in the light
of this late day; soft formless presences
move with the wind that sends a paper bag
scraping across the stones. A swirl of mist
hangs rags across the roofs. A severed tree
broods in my wonder that so much is lost
and yet so much persists to form again.
Stand freely here. Here one can look both ways,
knowing the world's attuned to that benign
forgotten music—in another time
than this tense moment beating wings to lift
and sheer towards related yesterdays.

CAVE

Roland Robinson

Battalions mass in the hills.
Sudden displacements of air
buffet the shack. Shrapnel
hammers the iron roof.

Odin's bolt, the Valkyries'
avalanche splits the sky.
The usurers, the war-lords,
move king, bishop, and pawn.

Götterdämmerung. The world
in ruins falls on our roof,
Hell's magnificent music,
our firelight in its heart.

The dog, Fenris, comes drenched,
bristling into the cave,
settles himself down among
rushes and hides on the floor.

Tonight's ten thousand years,
and the wolf growls in his sleep.
Firelight brings bison, deer,
thundering from the walls.

THE BOONGARY

David Campbell

In the night, they say, the boongary can be
heard walking in the trees—*Carl Sofus Lumholtz*

On Monday night I went to bed,
A snow-gum sprang from my sleeping head
By the banks of the Grubberdedrack.

On Tuesday night it grew so tall
Birds nested there and made their call
By the banks of the Grubberdedrack.

On Wednesday night an axeman came,
He said, I'll ringbark your snow-gum
By the banks of the Grubberdedrack.

On Thursday night the axe did crack
And turned on him like a tiger snake
By the banks of the Grubberdedrack.

On Friday night the white sun shone
At midnight in my green snow-gum
By the banks of the Grubberdedrack.

On Saturday night in my branching hair
Grey thrushes filled with song the air
By the banks of the Grubberdedrack.

On Sunday night while I lay at ease
The boongary walked within the trees
By the banks of the Grubberdedrack.

REFLECTIONS OF AN ARTIST

David Campbell

From my high room in hospital
That looked across the lake
I saw whole multitudes on wheels
Spin citywards and back.

Each morning mirrored in the lake
The slim gilled cars slid by
Of men who filled the office blocks
That on the water lay.

The amber city in the lake
Was shimmering when a wind
Sprang up and men and office blocks
Vanished out of mind.

In homes and lighted tenements
And bungalows of red
Shrill housewives stood about the doors
And swore their men were dead.

And dead they very well might be
Had I with brush and pen
And all the spaciousness of art
Not set them free again.

WINGS

Judith Wright

Between great coloured vanes the butterflies
drift to the sea with fixed bewildered eyes.

Once all their world was food; then sleep took
over,
dressed them in cloaks and furs for some great
lover—

some Juan, some Helen. Lifted on their dream
they rose and circled into heaven's slipstream

to seek each other over fields of blue.
Impassioned unions waited—can't-come-true

images. Blown, a message or a kiss,
earth sent them to the sun's tremendous Yes.

Once met and joined, they sank; complete and
brief
their sign was fastened back upon the leaf.

Empty of future now, the wind turned cold,
their rich furs worn, they thin to membraned
gold.

Poor Rimbauds never able to return
out of the searing rainbows they put on,

their wings have trapped them. Staring helplessly
they blow beyond the headland to the sea.

THE DEAD ASTRONAUT

Judith Wright

I circle still. You showed me love when time
    began;
and when this flesh had burned away, my bones
melted to nothing and eternity,
I cried to taste Time and your clay again.
I saw you veiled in air, impeccable Mary,
ageless Earth, clothed in old imagery.
There'd be no stone of you I would not kiss.

But I go blowing weightless in light's ways—
a hollow wingless seed, a seed of death—
and my eternity has no nights or days.
I circle you forever, visible Earth
who separate dark from light. You, you alone,
fabricate diamonds in your sightless stone
and make the universe into a truth.

Had I heart, eyes—as I am charred and blind—
I'd watch forever your altering light and dark,
your circling seasons, your renewing meaning—
those words I used! Do you know you focus there
all of this space, the dream of the dumb sleeper
who is the axis of the galaxies?
Because of you, for you alone
this terrible sun began his endless shining.

Give me your night. I burn.

TWO SIDES OF A STORY

Judith Wright

1. KENNEDY

That obstinate thoughtless proud
intelligent gay young man
read in his tent by night
from Leichhardt's Journal, and said
"I shall lead these tatterdemalion
convicts and rogues of mine
even through hell outright,
like this proud contrary German.
My heartbeat tells me I can."

Strata of ranges and rivers
stood between him and his vow.
The dark insulted spearmen
hid brooding their hate like lovers,
painted with clay and vermillion,
while the cartwheels dragged too slow
and the rain came down. But Kennedy,
that stubborn dogmatic proud
gay attractive young man,
held service every Sunday,
saw the right Lesson was read
and wrote up his Journal carefully.

Oh, see what it is to be born
sixth child of a regular Major
("of fine record")—and to learn
the disciplined trade of surveyor.
See what it is to be British,
poor, ambitious and gay,

with a name to be made, and a way
to find, and an admiration
for a rather impractical Leader.

Now, Edmund, Edmund Kennedy,
so sanguine, hopeful, vernal,
you travel to your infernal
and painfully humbling anguish
with a gentlemanly passion.
Revenge and slow starvation
have tattered your Expedition:
your sextant lost, and your Journal,
you die in the rain alone.

Or, if not alone, then nearly.
Though commendable, your companion
was only a savage. Dearly
as he cradled your head on his shoulder
from the exquisite grip of your pain,
you remembered public opinion,
your duty, the Expedition,
gave one last gasping order,
lifted your pencil to paper,
and died of your own ambition,
never speaking again.

II. JACKY JACKY

We see you still through a mist of sentiment,
Galmahra—Songman—born at a time unlucky,
in your tribe's last days, and you the last of their
    poets,
and doomed to be known by the nickname Jacky
    Jacky.

No one recorded the time and place of your birth;
but the white men had your country when you
　　were young
and called it Jerry's Plains. For what you were
　　worth,
they fed you scraps and taught you a humble
　　tongue.

No one recorded how you came to reach
Sydney Harbour from your country far on the
　　Hunter,
nor how you came to be listed as thirteenth man
on the solemn Expedition that crossed blue water.

What was it you came to feel for Edmund
　　Kennedy?
What was it looked out of your eyes at your gay
　　young Leader—
your gentle bottomless eyes?—as, grave and polite,
you cut a road for that heavy preposterous cart,
growing more indispensable as the way grew
　　harder.

"Faithful" was the word the newspapers used,
and the officials, raking the rags left over
from their hopeful Expedition to far Cape York—
the few starved bones and bits of harness-leather.
Faithful—the way these wretched blacks should
　　be,
but seldom are—a model for all your people,
who sit in the wurlies and mope and are un-
　　grateful
for our busy invasion and our civilized example.

They too must love and help us. So we gave you
a special medal to be worn for the rest of your
　　days,
and fifty pounds in the Bank for approved
　　expenses,
and we spoke of you with pleased, uneasy
　　surprise.

Yes, something, some faintly disgusted incredulity
clouded our commendation. How odd of Kennedy
to die on so black a breast, in arms so alien!
It seemed somehow to betray a lack of dignity.

But you, Galmahra? I try to see into your eyes,
as deep and obscure as the depths of your Hunter
　　River.
You must have loved him; you wept as you
　　buried him,
and you wept again, when your own escape was
　　over.

But why? I imagine you slowly gaining hope,
hope that increased as the Expedition failed:
knowing yourself the only trusted guide,
hoping that somehow the wound might now be
　　healed;

that the smouldering grief in your heart might
　　meet his eyes
and be quenched in their comforting blue; that
　　you both might ride
through that nightmare country, mutually for-
　　given,
black logical as white, and side by side.

Surely some word would come, some confirma-
tion
that you were now his treasure, his Expedition,
since all the others were treacherous, lost, or
dead.
He began to write — what message? — then
dropped his head.

Over its burning weight you started to weep.
You scarcely looked at the grouped half-hearted
spears
while his heavy head burned in. Not all your
tears
could put that pain out. It seared you terribly
deep.

In Maitland Hospital, after, you felt it burning,
a redhot weight. And cough as you might, it
stayed
till the day, years after, when drunk as a paid-up
drover
you fell in the campfire. Like an accepted lover
you clasped the flame in your arms and into your
heart
and died at last of an unacknowledged yearning.

Songmen may live their song, if they are lucky.
And you were Galmahra.

Or were you Jacky Jacky?

IN THE HUON VALLEY

James McAuley

Propped boughs are heavy with apples,
Springtime quite forgotten.
Pears ripen yellow. The wasp
Knows where windfalls lie rotten.

Juices grow rich with sun.
These autumn days are still:
The glassy river reflects
Elm-gold up the hill

And big white plumes of rushes.
Life is full of returns;
It isn't true that one never
Profits, never learns:

Something is gathered in,
Worth the lifting and stacking;
Apples roll through the graders,
The sheds are noisy with packing.

A WALK IN THE PARK

At Richmond, London

Rosemary Dobson

The world ran backwards, colour ebbed,
The falling leaves crashed down and died.
Mist rolled from Europe to engulf
The dun and dripping trees, my steps
Skirred on dead summer underneath.

Keeping the world beneath my feet
And all that glorious summer crushed
To husks, I paced the royal park.
Crystals and stars hung from the trees
And nuns and deer sprang from my way.

How strangely companied I was!
In all that Monday space and time
But nuns and deer! And which were which
Could hardly be determined—both
In twos and threes kept watch and ware.

With neat and nimble feet they leapt
Nervously from my blundering way
And though I held in metaphor
The bread of friendship in my hand
They kept their sidelong glance from me.

Wimpled and antlered, soft of eye,
Timorous, disciplined and quick
Through mazy mist and thorny boughs
Evasive still, on flying feet
They bounded, quivering, out of sight.

I did not care to sojourn there
Alone, unwanted, lumbering
In shaggy coat and heavy boots.
Rejected, raging, I came down
To find my fellows in the town.

SCENE: ALEXANDRA TEA ROOM

(A Provincial City, 1968)

Hal Porter

An East-of-Suez ceiling-fan, stopped dead
some hot, F. Scott Fitzgerald afternoon,
says ten-to-nevermore above your head
while you—you bitch!—and I do goodbye's deed,
stir stillborn tea with an unsilver spoon.

One other patron (naice) who's overheard
our nitric-acid truths, *art nouveau* lies
(two haters parting spare no hurting word),
in genteel autumn cocoa strives to hide
her White Queen's Church-of-England-coloured
    eyes.

If you and I were Alice we could climb
this nervy marble table-top and pass
into that other tea-room's Proustian time,
the Jabberwocky lovescape we disclaim,
the mimsy vistas through the looking-glass.

The White Queen *there*, all tousled shawl and
    hair,
would shrill that pins had pricked before they
    had,
and waste some grief on us who do not care
that love has cured to loathing, There to Here:
"I wish that you could manage to be glad."

Hal Porter

"Consider what o'clock it is," she'd plead.
Near shut-up time, the storm-chipped cups drunk
     dry,
too Tenniel for tears things run to seed.
Each city's full of cities. Hell's deployed.
All abysses are shallow. So am I.

"I first must hurt if I am to forgive."
Who says it? You. You fool! I'm silent stone
not snarling, "I'm indifferent that you live,"
and "I don't feel the wound you think you gave,"
or "*So*, that's *how you look when you're alone!*"

THE GARDEN

Geoffrey Dutton

All through the flowering months
                     the sunblink children
Flash their shadows
                     on flaring or frosty petals
And berries bouncing like robins
                     on boughs over fleshy leaves
That dive to earth-cool bulbs
                     and fat roots forked like thighs.
All's innocent
                     ancient and lovely as the classical names,
Narcissus, hellebore,
                     laburnum, anemone, delphinium,
Fresh and country-honest
                     as all the old English names,
Lords and ladies, foxglove,
                     henbane, nightshade, naked ladies.
And in their leaves, flowers,
                     little clicking seeds, plump berries,
Names also beautiful and old,
                     belladonna, andromedotoxin,
Delphinin, digitoxin, hyoscyamine,
                     juices that on children's tongues
Become violent delirium, anorexia,
                     mydriasis, diarrhoea, cyanosis,
Maniacal activity,
                     coma, mors, mortes, death, deaths.
Yet somewhere at the bottom of the garden
                     in the cottage with drooping gutters
Where the children are afraid to go,
                     the old witch, with her wood-stove's

Geoffrey Dutton

Bubbling burden of cast-iron pots
        and her ceiling like an inverted garden
Growing dry bunches of stalks and leaves,
        has simples and tinctures and purges
And powders of pounded roots
        that loosen the reins, discharge the gravel,
Dissolve the stone,
        and let you see your true-love in a dream.

FATHER AND CHILD

Gwen Harwood

1. BARN OWL

Daybreak: the household slept.
I rose before the sun.
A horny fiend, I crept
out with my father's gun.
Let him dream of a child
obedient, angel-mild—

old No-sayer, robbed of power
by sleep. I knew my prize
who swooped home at this hour
with daylight-riddled eyes
to his place on a high beam
in our old stables, to dream

light's useless time away.
I stood, holding my breath,
in urine-scented hay,
master of life and death,
a wisp-haired judge whose law
would punish beak and claw.

My first shot struck. He swayed,
ruined, beating his only
wing as I watched, afraid
by the fallen gun, a lonely
child who believed death clean
and final, not this obscene

bundle of stuff that dropped,
and dribbled through loose straw
tangling its bowels, and hopped

blindly closer. I saw
those eyes that did not see
mirror my cruelty

while the wrecked thing that could
not bear the light nor hide
hobbled in its own blood.
My father reached my side,
gave me the fallen gun.
"End what you have begun."

I fired. The blank eyes shone
once into mine, and slept.
I leaned my head upon
my father's arm, and wept
owl-blind in morning sun
for what I had begun.

2. NIGHTFALL

Forty years, lived or dreamed:
what memories pack them home.
Now the season that seemed
incredible is come.
Father and child, we stand
in time's long-promised land.

Since there's no more to taste,
ripeness is plainly all.
Father, we pick our last
fruits of the temporal.
Eighty years old, you take
this late walk for my sake.

Who can be what you were?
Link your dry hand in mine,
my stick-thin comforter.
Far distant suburbs shine
with great simplicities.
Birds crowd in flowering trees,

sunset exalts its known
symbols of transience.
Your passionate face is grown
to ancient innocence.
Let us walk for this hour
as if death had no power,

or were no more than sleep.
Things truly named can never
vanish from earth. You keep
a child's delight for ever
in birds, flowers, shivery-grass—
I name them as we pass.

"Be your tears wet?" You speak
as if air touched a string
near breaking-point. Your cheek
brushes on mine. Old King,
your marvellous journey's done.
Your night and day are one

as you find with your white stick
the path on which you turn
home with the child once quick
to mischief, grown to learn
what sorrows in the end
no words, no tears can mend.

DUST TO DUST

Gwen Harwood

I dream I stand once more
in Ann Street by the old
Fire Station. The palms
like feather dusters move
idly in stifling air.
The sky's dusted with gold.
A footfall: someone comes,
I cannot speak for love.

We walk in silence past
All Saints'. The dead do rise,
do live, do walk and wear
their flesh. Your exile's done.
So, so, resume our last
rejoicing kiss. Your eyes
flecked with my image stare
in wonder through my own.

Round us air turns to flame.
Ashes rain from the sky.
A firebell clangs and clangs
insanely as I wake
to absence. With your name
shaping my mouth I lie
losing the dream that hangs
fading in light, I shake

the last of night away.
These bright motes that define
morning inside my room
hold not one grain of you.

Another sunstruck day
whose stirring dust-motes shine
remote from any dream
cannot restore, renew

our laughter that hot night
when by All Saints' we talked
in the brief time we had—
during *Magnificat*
an urchin stopped to write
on the stone wall, and chalked
the message: GOD IS MAD.
I say Amen to that.

FAMILY HAPPINESS

J. R. Rowland

Family happiness
A theme not much explored
Left aside as lacking
Conflict, movement, stress—

Instead, the pangs of search
Among people who seldom seem
To marry, have regular jobs
Or go to dentist or church

And are rarely over thirty.
Falling in and out of love
In a kind of prolonged weekend
They don't pay bills, wash dirty

Socks, mend plugs, mow lawns
Nor cut the children's lunches
But drink whisky or campari
Converse in restaurants

Or agonize alone
On a range of subjects that
Leaves untouched what you
Or I flinch from as our own

Inmost fear or distress.
The world of novels is
Autonomous, it seems.
That it does not come too close

May be just as well
When, the children being in bed,
I see your reading head
In the quiet of lightfall

Your eye stumble, and quick
Pierce mine with a glance
Where something unbearable rises
Trembles and sinks back.

WINTER MATINS

R. F. Brissenden

Morning can be the best time of the day:
        Outside our window now
Cotoneasters catch the pale new light.
        Each crimson-berried bough
Glitters with frost, blood-bright against the blue
        And empty air. The sun
Flashes on emerald wings: king parrots swoop
        And settle, one by one.
Companionable, comically grave,
        Ruffled against the cold
They eat the brilliant fruit. Some hang head down-
        wards, spread slow wings to hold
Their swaying balance: in the softening air
        Their under-feathers burn
A clearer red, their wings a leafier green.
        Beauty and grace are born
Suddenly from the random movements of
        Birds. The incredulous heart
Stirs at the mystery, yearning still to find
        In chance the signs of art
And order. Quietly, warm from our bed
        Where you still sleep, I watch
The birds, remembering the love we made
        Last night; and wish that each
Day could begin like this, when simple joy
        Assumes the shape of praise
And prayer—as in that earliest and lost
        Morning of all our days.

THE MARRIAGE: BECCAFICOS

Grace Perry

They were the small birds greedy for fig-trees
whirring dark oceans to island groves.
They were the fat birds, heavy with ripe figs,
fallen like fruit and bottled in rows.

In pairs without protest, they gaze at the future
obscured by spices and sweetness and glass.
Each sadly deplores the companion withering,
awaiting the one hand that will not pass.

Slow salt and weak acid, the ritual recipe
hardens the flesh and softens the bones,
the cold syrup shrivelling visions of fig-trees,
the perilous flight with the flock, yet alone.

In the quiet house, they sit at the table,
living arrested without a word.
The fingers are subtle, from plate to mouth—
one movement, one swallow—the complete bird.

E

THE DEITY

from Aboriginal Carvings

Nancy Keesing

> At Cottage Point
> He is outlined on stone;
> Stiff rays round His head,
> He outstares the sun.
> He is fifteen feet long,
> His legs like saplings, stout.
> He is no god for Doubt,
> Guilt, Will or Benison.
> He is old, old, old and cut deep.
> I feel He is God.
>
> In a stuffy room
> Filled with breath and prayer
> God is a scroll
> God is a lion;
> You cannot see Him there,
> The fierce, loving spirit
> Which we inherit
> With all the ancient lore.
> Though worship chants on
> I think He has gone
>
> As also from the rock
> Since none now knows
> His nature or his fee.
> To Him no one can pray;
> Him none reject or choose,

His chosen are vanished,
All their days finished,
But He cannot lose
Himself for he is cut
Too deep in rock for that.

SWAN

David Rowbotham

Only in the waters of death, they say—
I have heard only the story,
Not your song, and in my riverless country
Never a swan—does the plumed spray
Of the psalm that is dawn by evening, eerie,
Being the first and last, or beautiful but wintry

Being sweetest in the oldest hour,
From your throat that is longer-stemmed than a
        lily
Stem forth like all the waters of the rivers
Awakening to their springs, and flower.
I have not heard it, but, newly
I listen hearing the songs of all thanksgivers

Who withhold, in the ageing silence of years,
The passions of purity and waiting
Till the greater departing passion of arrival
Releases the voice that gives and bears
Gentility and splendour's greeting.
Where you have sung there are some who rage
        and shuffle

Believing that they are mortal, less
Than death among the widening waters,
Not seeing that winter and wintry rivers gather
Season and volume back to their source,
To a spring like every swan which shatters
Darkness with dawn and the rock with the plume,
        thanksgiver.

THE GLOBE

Margaret Irvin

Where the children play beyond the gentle
    stresses
of our thoughts, out in the light
of the soft spring day among the last of winter
    grasses,
with bruises of winter lichen still in sight—

there is a globe so frail it quakes at the touch of
    shadows,
a sphere where danger and joy are spun.
Sunshine holds it together with hoops the colour
    of rainbows.
It focuses the equinoctial sun.

The children bend and straighten, move off or
    are still
in its scope. They are unaware
of the globe's diameter and the perilous angle
of radiance aimed from zero heights of air.

And they are not safe or free or stationary at all,
but prisoners in a centrifugal cage.
Above their unheeding heads universes tumble,
and round their shoulders translucent gulf-streams
    merge.

And we could lose them to this vast radiance,
and ethereal currents sweep them away.
But lightly, lightly the globe returns them to us
and the turf and clods that firm the close of day.

THE WIDOW

Joan Mas

The widow who lives in a house at the end of the
    street
              has a lover
And an illegitimate child. She is fenced about by
    the long,
              sharp tongues of people.
Every day a new picket is added to the fence.
Neighbours have a way of extending it. Women,
    over tea-cups.
              Men, over garden-walls.
That the widow has found an exit in the fence
    and walks
              through it
With the child, indicates a weakness in its struc-
    ture. Some
              faltering of will, by someone . . .
              somewhere,
Has made a gap between pickets.
The widow who never glances at people, keeps
    them suspiciously
              glancing at one another.

SNOWBOUND

(*from* Car)

Alexander Craig

Minutely inspecting the mooncold white
behind the motel,
I notice a furtive red and yellow
flickering across its slope,
thrown from the foot-high letters on the entrance,
  spelling
VACANCY.
The glass on the beige plasterboard wall
films me back-to-front for two days
in phantom 3D colour: I remain unselfconscious.
My tongue licks the filling protruding from a
  broken tooth.
I contemplate a crust of ice and a thin blue
  shadow
wedged between the window's parallel twin
  panes. I reflect
on the feel of the car's vinyl and even my bones,
  my fingers
releasing and gripping the steering-wheel.
I think of the ice on the bridges, the ice
under the culverts, the New York Thruway
"out solid" still (they say), the dead in their
  automobiles
discovered by bulldozers and the immeasurable
  drift of the snow.

SEAHORSES

Peter Porter

When we were children
We would cheer to find a seahorse
Among the wrack the breakers lifted
On to the beach. Sometimes two or three were
    together,
A team to pull a chariot of cuttle
Or like a suicide wreathed in fine
Sea ivy and bleached sea roses
One stiff but apologetic in its trance.
Seahorses were vikings—
Somewhere they impassively
Launched on garrulous currents
Seeking a far grave: wherever
That was, they set their stallion
Noses to it, ready to be garnered
In the sea's time at the sea's pleasure.
If we wondered why we loved them
We might have thought
They were the only creatures which had to die
Before we could see them—
In this early rule of death we'd recognize
The armorial pride of head, the unbending
Seriousness of small creatures,
Credit them with the sea's rare love
which throws them to us in their beauty,
Unlike the vast and pitiable whale
Which must be quickly buried for its smell.

THE HISTORY OF MUSIC

Peter Porter

Though this is not in Hesiod
Music was stolen from a God:

Not fire but notes the primal giver
Paid for with helpings of his liver

And virtuosi of the earth
Outsang the Gods who gave them birth.

When Orpheus plays we meet Apollo,
When there's theology to swallow

We set it to music, our greatest art,
One that's both intellect *and* heart,

There war and peace alike depict us
(Drums and trumpets in the Benedictus)—

It sang beneath the Grecian boat,
It kept Pythagoras afloat,

It suffered poets, critics, chat
And will no doubt survive Darmstadt;

This brandy of the damned of course
To some is just a bottled sauce,

Its treasons, spoils and stratagems
Aleatory as women's hems

Yet beauty who indulged the swan
At death completes her with a song

And Paradise till we are there
Is in these measured lengths of air.

THE SADNESS OF THE CREATURES

Peter Porter

We live in a third floor flat
among gentle predators
and our food comes often
frozen but in its own shape
(for we hate euphemisms
as you would expect) and our cat's
food comes in tins, other than
scraps of the real thing and she
like a clever cat makes milk
of it for her kittens: we shout
of course but it's electric
like those phantom storms
in the tropics and we think of
the neighbours—I'm not
writing this to say how guilty
we are like some well-paid
theologian at an American
College on a lake
or even to congratulate
the greedy kittens who have
found their mittens and are up
to their eyes in pie—I know
lots of ways of upsetting
God's syllogisms, real
seminar-shakers some of them,
but I'm a historical cat
and I run on rails and so
I don't frame those little poems
which take three lines to
get under your feet—
you know the kind of thing—

The water I boiled the lobster in
is cool enough to top
up the chrysanthemums.
No, I'm acquisitive and have
one hundred and seven Bach
Cantatas at the last count,
but these are things of the spirit
and my wife and our children
and I are animals (biologically
speaking) which is how the world
talks to us, moving on the billiard
table of green London, the sun's
red eye and the cat's green eye
focusing for an end. I know
and you know and we all know
that the certain end of each of us
could be the end of all of us,
but if you asked me what
frightened me most, I wouldn't
say the total bang or even
the circling clot in the red drains
but the picture of a lit room
where two people not disposed
to quarrel have met so
oblique a slant of the dark
they can find no words for
their appalled hurt but only
ride the rearing greyness:
there is convalescence from this,
jokes and love and reassurance
but never enough and never
convincing and when the cats
come brushing for food their soft

aggression is hateful;
the trees rob the earth and the earth
sucks the rain and the children
burgeon in a time of invalids—
it seems a trio sonata
is playing from a bullock's
skull and the God of Man
is born in a tub of entrails;
all man's regret is no more
than Attila with a cold
and no saviour here or
in Science Fiction will come
without a massacre of the innocents
and a rape of El Dorado.

AFTER MANY CAMPAIGNS, THE REUNION

Noel Macainsh

There are several versions of music
   and various evenings—
      in which men will make war.
Loving one to sweeten the other.
We see it in birds
   that make earth seem bound
      yet goad us to fly—
   having us purchase peace
      or the relief from it.

But treasure we our friends
   solely in hazard,
   the more they part into death
      or we into desolation?
   having extremes subtend the perspective
      of what is most real,
   as signs mean most
      only to those most lost—
   all meaning the other
      to where it is we seem most bound?

For here at the pole
   we remember the homeland
And at the homeland
   we remember the pole
And the inbetween-land
   is the passage of music—
      not the first phrase
         nor the last phrase
   but the various versions—

Noel Macainsh

contraries
  mingling in a continuing passage—
  birds and wars
  irreality and extremes
as in a marriage
the true bond stays fully
nor crumbles with the bone.

FIFTH ANNIVERSARY

Laurence Collinson

I need to share a petulance,
to fulminate with petty song
against my sad extravagance:
a love affair gone on too long.

Can a wounded stone reject
air's tender imbecility?
Unarmoured, how can I deflect
such terrible fidelity?

This shrivelled mountebank, this love
who juggles me and me and me,
wielding with his wilting glove
my lost and frequent liberty,

would, if he knew, implore his palm
to break my balanced impotence,
negotiating, calm by calm,
the orbit of my eloquence.

We have no silence to convert
our love, and must embrace aloud:
I in my transitory shirt,
my father in his fraying shroud.

DIVER

R. A. Simpson

Alone on the tower
I'm not confident.
The water is black
And distant.

I think of style
And raise my arms and aim,
Holding back the plunge.
It's mostly a game

That touches terror,
Then terror goes—
I view my fingers,
My toes.

"Defiance, love and revolt
Make the diver dive
And prove, through dying,
He's alive,"
A voice preaches in my head . . .

And so I dive.

Water gulps me down,
Chilling me with its grip,
Then arms pine up and up
Like worship.

SAND

Charles Higham

You can make castles of it, construct
The flying buttresses, gold cannons, where
Wind beats down from the sad Pacific—

Make the tall walls elegant and straight,
Carve slits to watch through as the army comes
With stealthy tread across the white, ribbed
    strand.

Set on the top a thin and tossing flag—
Let it crack bravely like a gun's report
Snapping straight, its linen pressed by breeze

And put the writhing seahorses down
On the drawbridge made of bits of wood from a
    ship—
Dig out an even moat for the sea to gurgle in.

And finally, when at dusk after a day of labour
You are done, stand naked in the centre,
The only time you can be a warrior—

Braving the sea's clashing shields to ride
You down, your gawk arms raw, a rusted spade
Clutched in your hand, and a drum of heat

Rapped in your chest till the bold green quiets it.

SITTINGS BY APPOINTMENT ONLY

Bruce Beaver

Some days I feel like a not-so-big
Nest of chairs.
People take me apart just to sit
On top of me
The easier to listen and look at others
Or rest themselves.
Then when the recital's over
I'm left fragmented
For something like a janitor to stack
Me back in my place,
One structure of many pieces.
One day I swear
I'll lock myself together or learn
The knack of collecting
My self in mid-performance and sandwich them:
Captives of the tower,
Cuckoo-guests of my nest of chairs.

THE WANDERER

Bruce Beaver

On Manly Wharf one autumn afternoon,
April or May, some fifty years ago
Chris Brennan stood and watched the setting sun
Perform, applauding in its afterglow.
This was his mentor of the heavenly host;
This often bilious, always brilliant one
That boxed his burning ears and struck the lost
Chord of the planets—Not that Lilith moon
That glossed his nights and pointed through the
    deep
Blue of his days a forefinger of bone.
And so he turned his huge eyes to the west,
And supplicating watched the god go down
Into the dragon depths. The night was vast
With scattered shoals of stars nibbling at sleep.

POET'S LIFE AND LOVES

Bruce Beaver

Two years old already
The latest anthology withers
Beneath its plastic cover
Upon his reading table.
He enters without blinking
That ghetto of contenders,
That race apart of poets;
Sees in every window,
In each shop-front's reflection,
In every bar-room mirror
In each and every puddle
Or retinal rejoinder
Square-on, up-gazing, lowering
His own fantastic features.
Whirling past the index
In fugal introspection
He exits without knocking.
Convinced of his out-going
He spends the day unwinding
With Pelicans and Penguins.
The former bring his beak-fuls
Of fry and bitter water;
Surrounding him, the latter
Leave small stones in his keeping.
He knows he is accepted.
They understand him, almost.
Quaint and harsh the chorus
Of their farewells, as, tearful,
He sails into the sunset
Upon a plastic cover,
Upon his reading table,
Too old, too altogether.

I. M. KENNETH MACKENZIE

Cambridgeshire 1967

Evan Jones

If I look up to watch the water stream
    Down the plate-glass, and down among the trees
    The water of the moat a muddy gleam
Cutting us off from the rich meadow-leas,
    I think of you, Mackenzie, twelve years dead:
    It seems unkind that none of this can please
The waking eye that in your late life read
    The play of light and leaves, the flight of birds,
    With such live comprehension. Now, instead,
I sit here huddled in my nest of words
    Imagining how you would see it all:
    Two acres that a shallow moat still guards
From the encroaching bungalows, a wall
    Ruined between the lawn and rougher ground
    Where in long grass cock pheasants strut and
        call—
Lesser birds always fill the air with sound—
    And this old row of stables, now become
    A house as handsome as I ever found.
England and England's weather. Here the Cam
    Flows calm and shallow between grassy banks,
    Wandering to its city in a dream
Of other Aprils; here the church-bell thanks
    All seasons for nine hundred years of stone;
    Here a half-timbered and thatched village flanks
A winding side-road: here we are alone
    In country-side that Wordsworth might have
        scanned
    Or Byron galloped through, or Milton known,

Evan Jones

Deep in the shire for men who understand,
    A shire of various weathers, where today
    A rainy stillness softens all the land
That golden stillness softened yesterday—
    All this to make you envious, and then
    London is less than fifty miles away,
The great heart of the language, the great wen
    That poets always flocked to to achieve
    The recognition that you have not won.

Jobless, romantic, how you wished to leave
    Australia, where you drank too much, you said,
    Because your talent starved there; I believe
You must have half-believed it: but instead
    You washed up broken on a mountain-side
    Where at long last earth, trees and water fed
An eye for innocence before you died,
    Bringing self-knowledge and serenity
    That time can neither injure nor deride.
Now and in England, nothing that I see
    Can equal that: and having come to that
    It is unthinkable that you might be
Pleased or encouraged by the pit-a-pat
    Of literary London. And what else
    Could England offer that you had not got,
Who had the language beating in your pulse,
    The history in your bones, as strong and clear
    As here the poets have them thin and false?
England and England's weather. Everywhere
    The post-card scenery is giving way,
    The fabric crumbling, unless special care
Is being taken that will make it pay:
    Here every second cottage sells "Antiques".
    One slashes through it on the motor-way

Living between the throttle and the brakes,
    Registering the blank submissiveness
    Of all that's old to all that's new and fake,
Creating a pervasive ugliness
    That, unbelievable though it may seem,
    Flatters our own suburban wilderness—
From here I hear the bulldozer's gruff scream
    Faintly across the moat and through the trees;
    The council houses swell up in a dream.
I sit here in my nest of words at ease,
    Knowing that I shall not be here for long
    And perfectly secure of my own peace.

It must have been like this at Kurrajong.

SNAPSHOTS FOR MARGOT

Evan Jones

One of those Carlton parties: beer or claret
(Acid and cheap), three times as many people
As the two rooms could comfortably hold;
In tie and jacket, feeling rather old,
I sat there talking to a former pupil.
You moved across the threshold and stood near it.

Our conversations lingered over salad.
Married in May (with bridesmaid and best man:
Dark-suited me, and you superb in white),
For seven days we watched the evening light
Ebb from the Derwent valley; on the high plain
We drove through early winter pure and pallid.

In France, we took hot water in a bucket
Up to the bidet where we bathed our baby,
Put her to bed, and then went down to dine.
You crunched the bones of little birds; the wine
Was cheap and sharp; our room was rather
    shabby.
We loved it all and had seen nothing like it.

Pregnant again already, now you move
In and about the house (beneath the boughs,
Over the stove); our daughter sits and babbles
Or crawls like a crab under the chairs and tables
While I sit reading, brooding, seeing you as
My love, my bride, my wife, and still my love.

A MAN TALKS TO HIMSELF

J. M. Couper

Used to the bitter pleasure, these winter nights,
of watching, beside the fire, in comfort, in a
chair,
death after dinner conveyed in harmless shots
with background music to civilize the war.

Wears us mature as a nation. Cool reporter.
Any day's choicest catastrophes quite without
bias,
though war is of course a patriotic disaster
ending at last in peace in Martin Place.

But peaceful protests become barbarities.
The marcher puts on frightfulness, copies the
soldier,
storms town halls and parliaments armed with his
voice.

Peace thrives like the throaty rattle of our own
G.I.s
on the edge of the Mekong River, in the civil
clutter,
dying to put some flesh on political chimeras.

THE PLACE

Bruce Dawe

The day I happened upon that still place
I'd got my hair cut by a friend whose mediaeval
    humour it was
To cut haywire and then walk in pure friendship
Down Collins Street with me, in as broad-minded
    a daylight
As you'll find in this city on Sunday, grinning
    sidelong like a gun
At his handiwork, the gapped nape of my neck
Where his crooked hand-clippers had bitten
Deep as a skull in a dream. *O, I turned all heads
    that were turnable*
That day, between Swanston and Russell
And I couldn't get home quick enough
To hold up a round shaving-mirror over my head
Like a silver third eye which would reveal to me
What all the world knew. . . .

                Then it was—just then
—I came upon it, in retrospect: the place of
    baldness,
That solemn high country some get to earlier
    than others
And some not at all. It was like being on top of a
    hill whistling
With wind, and seeing the green lone grass
Parting under the brush and sweep of it, seeing
    how the world
Wears thin at last under the constant abrasion of
    skies,
The perpetual combing of clouds.

               In that place of revelation

I forgave my friend's innocent butchery,
And had I possessed two heads would gladly have
     proffered him one
To work on until he was perfect,
And I peered down on myself from that mirrored
     height,
Rejoicing quietly at the double-barbering flood
On whose littered waters I bobbed with all of
     mankind,
Being grateful for such a reminder,
So early on in the piece. . . .

EASY DOES IT

Bruce Dawe

I have to be careful with my boy.
When he says tree it comes out hazy
very green and friendly and before I've got
the meaning straight he's up there laughing in it,
or working on the word for aeroplane
which is also a little above his head
so that he has to stand on tiptoe to touch it
—for him it does Immelmanns to order,
but when I try it becomes suddenly
only a model in a museum with props that slowly
    turn
when the button is pushed and a cutaway section
to show the engine in action. . . .
I have to be careful with my boy,
that I don't crumple his immediate-delivery-
    genuine-fold-up-and-extensible-world
into correct English forever, petrify its wonder
with the stone gaze of grammar, or turn him into
a sort of Sunday visitor at the lakeside
who brings bags of specially-prepared bread-
    crusts
to feed to swans who arch their necks and hiss.

HOME-COMING

Bruce Dawe

All day, day after day, they're bringing them
home,
they're picking them up, those they can find, and
bringing them home,
they're bringing them in, piled on the hulls of
Grants, in trucks, in convoys,
they're zipping them up in green plastic bags,
they're tagging them now in Saigon, in the
mortuary coolness
they're giving them names, they're rolling them
out of
the deep-freeze lockers—on the tarmac at Tan
Son Nhut
the noble jets are whining like hounds,
they are bringing them home
—curly-heads, kinky-hairs, crew-cuts, balding
non-coms
—they're high, now, high and higher, over the
land, the steaming *chow mein*,
their shadows are tracing the blue curve of the
Pacific
with sorrowful quick fingers, heading south,
heading east,
home, home, home—and the coasts swing up-
ward, the old ridiculous curvatures
of earth, the knuckled hills, the mangrove
swamps, the desert emptiness . . .
in their sterile housing they tilt towards these
like skiers
—taxiing in, on the long runways, the howl of
their home-coming rises

surrounding them like their last moments (the
    mash, the splendour)
then fading at length as they move
on to small towns where dogs in the frozen
    sunset
raise muzzles in mute salute,
and on to cities in whose wide web of suburbs
telegrams tremble like leaves from a wintering
    tree
and the spider grief swings in his bitter geometry
—they're bringing them home, now, too late, too
    early.

LISTENING TO T'ANG POETRY

at the time of the Viet Nam war

Norman Talbot

Maybe the bones of that poet
all eleven hundred years long
have been combed out by winds
of opposed & harrowing seasons
      across the ribs of China
the clanging gorges underneath Chung-Nan . . .

& nearer always maybe the gibbeted exile
swings over desperate taxed fields
accountable in silver & aluminum
& over each year's bright developing
      weapons of the soldiers
carried loosely but of course bright
& worn smooth—renewable as spring—

& always maybe the peasant's back
knots to a hoop & the woodcutter
piously trussed to a thousandyear technique
      of drudgery always maybe
      chews his bare datestone
& sees his axehandle rotted in the wind.

BALMORAL, SUMMER

Vivian Smith

All day the weight of summer and the shrill
spaced flight of jet planes climbing north.
The news at half past twelve brought further
    crimes.
Insane dictators threaten new disasters.

The light of summer with its bone white glare
and pink hibiscus in the yacht club garden.
The beach is strewn with bodies of all sizes.
How the sight of human nudity surprises—
cleft buttock, shaved arm-pit, nipple hair.

The heat haze hovers over Grotto Point
and skiers skim the violent flat water.
Incredible the feats that art demands.

Submarines surface to refuel
around this headland in a small bay's stillness.
History encroaches like an illness.
And children chase the gulls across the sand.

ALLIES OF NATURE

Chris Wallace-Crabbe

All our bright shops and autumn-dapple streets
   Are bustling with sunlit women,
Custodians of reality;

Mothers and wives, our fair bright flames, they go
   Without a haven or a den,
Looking to Caesar's coin, Caesar's food,

And shepherding the children in their zoo,
   Little bear, small tiger, white mouse:
Life is tough out there, and they know it.

They know the world has conspired against them,
   That men spin shoddy morals from
The cobwebs of a spurious law,

That men are stung by spontaneity
   And, being hurt, must creep away
Down to their books, up to windy schemes.

Out of a chaos of abstractions now
   We reach for you in quest of light,
Dear flesh guiding us, our bitter loves:

You show your teeth, you come out spitting chips,
   Cutting through legalistic tape
With your bloody innocence of heart,

Well aware, yes, having known all along
   Which sex it is wires up Auschwitz,
Brews a new gas, murders the Kulaks. . . .

Chris Wallace-Crabbe

Okay, stand up! Stand up, Lysistrata,
   But keep your little purse away,
Hidden from the mad rogues and their guns;

Be yourself, be irrational, be fierce
   To resist the impossible
Grand construction, glittering out

In tiers of cone and cube and cylinder
   Airy-high in the moonlit fog,
As hollow as half a memory.

Eyes flashing, lips parted, stand there and cry
   Against the cutting-edge of mind
Cleaving nothing but air in its rage

For impersonal order: stop it short.
   Let feeling flourish like a wood,
Burgeoning, tangling, spattered with sun,

To struggle and grope without constriction,
   Twigs budding, great boughs bearing down
And old trunks falling to rot below:

It is this you want, ladies, and of course
   It does you credit, beautiful
Allies of nature that you all are.

Indeed, I cannot resist you; I yield
   To the force of your attractions
And the quick truths you assault me with,

Keeping my reservations to myself.

HELL

Chris Wallace-Crabbe

A past without a present
this is Hell.

A future inaccessible
running through wet fingers,

an open hourglass full of rain,
the cyclone coursing through a fishnet,

prophecy greasily sliding
into the vats of history:

no contact, no action,
this is Hell.

The wet ball eludes our groping hands
bouncing for ever down a black wind-tunnel,

bumpety-bump, one field of grope and slide;
the clockface shot to bits

which fly in all our eyeballs
melting like snowflakes,

future without a present,
Cassandra's tape-recorder whirling round

as round and round we go
singing old school songs.

Chris Wallace-Crabbe

Rain falling in the sea
while autumn trash ochres the jonquil-beds,

a sort of monstrous Eden,
this is Hell.

SIGNS

Chris Wallace-Crabbe

However strict the flame below refinement,
Contours of art take colour from the world
And, after Hitler made his contribution
To the wintry bonfire of aesthetics,
Degenerate art on show like a zoo in Munich,
Heavy butchers mocking at their mockers,
I like to think of Paul Klee quietly painting
Small black signs on panels full of sunlight
In a cool hinterland of peace,
Already with the seeds of death inside him,
The seeds of that selfsame, ash-coloured tree
That laid its long black shadows over Europe
And burned for five years after he was dead
Who is not dead, but living in clear colour.

HEAVEN, IN A WAY

Rodney Hall

From my new world I'm waving.
See how far I've come?
Here it's perfectly all right
to turn however many somersaults you like
on all the roofs of town.
If anyone should care to live
in Gothic or in Romanesque cathedrals
that's alright too: you spread
your palliasse upon the altar or in the nave
and wake to find the morning sun
shattered to a flower of jewelled glass—
to find the ghost of a multicoloured
saint or two in bed beside you.

From my new world I'm waving.
See how far I've come?
It's no use being envious;
nothing but a life of heartbreak
can win you entry to this place.
Here the fish are naturally disguised
with scales that read as Hebrew letters.
The smells of every intimate remembrance
play your mind on their hook and line, until you
    do
achieve a state of re-experience.
And the colours here lie warm against the eye:
film upon film of unforgotten pleasure.

I suppose it's heaven, in a way.
And I am waving down at you.
Ha ha! I hope you hate it where you are.

I see you—a grubby speck beneath me,
and it's all your own damned fault.
You don't know what you're missing.
Watch me exploit the magic
of my somersaulting powers. Up here
we're worshippers of education by experience;
with only another life of heartbreak still to go
before we accept ourselves, each as one of you.
From my new world I'm waving.
See how far I've come?

DIALOGUE

Philip Martin

No God, none, she said. And he said: Love
Is God. I pray, when I come in at your gates
You catch at the saint's experience: all an out-
    flowing,
A flowing-together, confounding of words. She
Drew him in closer. His voice, quick, ran on;
Here was the resurrection, in their flesh,
God's very breath. Dear love, to me, she said,
All this means nothing. Thrust in against me,
    hard.

FLYING FOX

Thomas W. Shapcott

She tosses and rumples alone on the double bed:
when, damn him, when will his car cringe in
through their gate and clatter over the one loose
    stone
to announce his coming? Her life has become a
    code
of sound, a mesh of reassurances
and locks. She wills herself still and tight. No use,
each minute drums with the wrong silence, the
    wrong noise
on the rigid tendons of her own unease.

And still she waits, as tensely she listens, and hears
in the rank-growing neighbour papaw-tree outside
a marauding flying-fox circle and flap and cling
scooping the ripe air, gripping with clawed wings
at its easy quarry, the fleshy neglected fruit,
and tear through its shallow skin, and feast on it.

THE CARP

(after Joachim Ringelnatz)

David Malouf

In their lighted restaurant tank,
as in an aquarium
for rare and privileged monsters,
the carp. Their flesh is ragged,
a trifle beaten-up
from contact with fishmongers.
Inside they shine and flash.

Bearded like T.V. wizards,
they mumble spells; speech-bubbles
trail from their blunt heads, clearing
the element; they dream
of razors—being shaved
and gutted, warmed, dressed up
to the gills in mayonnaise.

Their resting-place a tycoon's
belly, leaving a bone,
a small parting protest,
lodged in his throat.
When I think of their souls I see
woodlice doing knee-bends
in rows like ballet-girls. . . .

Found little else in Melbourne
to astonish, or distress.

From THE TESTAMENT OF TOURMALINE

Variations on Themes of the TAO TEH CHING

Randolph Stow

I

The loved land breaks into beauties, and men
    must love them
with tongues, with words. Their names are sweet
    in the mouth.

But the lover of Tao is wordless, for Tao is nameless:
Tao is a sound in time for a timeless silence.

Loving the land, I deliver my mind to joy;
but the love of Tao is passionless, unspoken.

Nevertheless, the land and Tao are one.
In the love of the land, I worship the manifest Tao.

To move from love into lovelessness is wisdom.
The land's roots lie in emptiness. There is Tao.

V

    A smith at work
does not consult the iron.
    Passionless, silent,
he forms it to his pattern.

    Forge-flames leap
in fragile multiplicity,
    changed, renewed
by the breath of the empty bellows.

97

What can be empty
yet ever and all replenishing?
Under the bellows
blazes the world's forge-fire.

VII

The loved land will not pass away.
World has no life but transformation.
Nothing made selfless can decay.
The loved land will not pass away.

The grown man will not pass away.
Body is land in permutation.
Tireless within the fountains play.
The grown man will not pass away.

VIII

Grown men are water,
seeking the basins,
close to the darkness,
feeding the land.

A mud-brick house
for a heart of silence,
yielding in friendship,
unveiling in speech.

Grown men are water
and uncontending.
Rooted in darkness.
Feeding the land.

WESTERN WIND WHEN WILL THOU BLOW

Randolph Stow

Five nights in love, five nights we lay:
the sea of the Hebrides rocked the bay.

The wind of the Hebrides shook the slates,
the dank sheep coughed at the paddock gates.

Five firelit nights, five dawns on snow
the glamour held. "Don't go, don't go."

Upon your heels, as you stepped furth,
a great still frost seized all the earth.

Till quiet, quiet the glazed sea swells,
the land is cast of cattle-bells;

like shattered windows hoarding fire
the cracked lochs lie. Ice spikes the byre.

Green flames of driftwood walk my night.
The starving deer look in, take fright.

In frost is death. Love, love to bring
the storm, the thaw, the spate, the spring

—the sea of the Hebrides wild with air,
the wind of the Hebrides on the stair.

THROUGH DARKENED SUBURBS

Craig Powell

Rain on the street after a dwindling storm.
From the car window all the houses might
dissolve like stars, and fluid street lamps form
a language of their pale colloquial light.

Drive slowly and the car noise falls away.
Moonlit cats drip softly over fences
into the delicate shadows of their grey
world, a world of sudden dazzling glances

cutting your headlights. Here you are estranged,
a home of people you will never meet,
and yet you'll bear this substance of the street

deeply to move within your blood at last,
and know these people must awake unchanged
unaware that anyone has passed.

HANOVER STREET

Andrew Taylor

The flags strain stiff as plywood in the wind—
over the continent it seems to have come
to drive its chill into my finger-joints
and numb their progress over the blank page.
The planes, re-routed so they pass above
in the white wind, strain audibly to land,
the uncurled clouds drive silently, steadily on;
no rain, no premonition of rain, just wind
and cold. A pepper-tree flings like a boa,
two pencil cypresses tight as a spring contrive
to sway stiffly, uneasily, but they sway—
their acknowledgement to the season. Only grey
stone sawn crudely into blocks stands straight
and stubbornly upright, earth's element
rooted against its old antagonist.

The builder and the architect who raised
this grey colonial house, as burgherly
as a warehouse, and most fashionable once,
traced in its lines an elegance of strength,
a confidence that what it stood for was right,
against the cold air blowing day in, day out.

WALLACE STEVENS

Peter Skrzynecki

I

Among old text books and holy pictures
The skull has been kept for ten years now,
Wrapped in white silk, hidden away.

The lagoon was knee-deep in faint light
Around the edges where we were prawning.
Ten years ago, washed up on the inlet—

Well-hidden under rocks and water lily;
Recovered next morning and carried
Back in secret, never to be shared.

II

Taken out, year after year, held up
To a lamp and revolved: revolved
While light washed the dome, flawless, cleaner.

In ten years only the beak has changed:
Fallen to one side, membrane unevenly
Parted as if in annoyance or fear: splayed.

III

No winds, sand or speared fish become part
Emblems of that night, of nets and sea weed,
Of that gull—caught, washed from what coast?

Not even the angels of ten years ago
To whom the psalms were offered nightly:

Only shells, with their trapped music,
Soft, stiletto.

BACHELOR FARMER

Roger McDonald

At half-past five—the earth cooling,
All the sweat of his shirt
Soaked up in red dirt—
He tunnels his arm through the weight
Of a bag of wheat, slowly withdraws it,
And sees how the yellow grains
Shiver, as though magnetized away
From his skin, each one alone and trembling.

Walking beside the fence, in another paddock,
He discovers a grain
Caught in the hairs of his wrist:
He bends down, allows it to fall,
And with the careful toe of his boot
Presses it into the ground.

Sleeping all night, sprawled on the veranda of his
    hut,
He wakes to the call of the pallid cuckoo,
Its blunted scale
Low on the heads of unharvested wheat—

Not rising towards him, not falling away,
But close by, unchanging, incomplete.

ONCE IN A LIFETIME, SNOW

Les A. Murray

for Chris and Mary Sharah
Winters at home brought wind,
Black frost and raw
Grey rain in barbed wire fields,
But never more

Until the day my uncle
Rose at dawn
And stepped outside—to find
His paddocks gone,

His cattle to their hocks
In ghostly ground
And unaccustomed light
For miles around.

And he stopped short, and gazed
Lit from below,
And half his wrinkles vanished
Murmuring "Snow...."

A man of farm and fact
He stared to see
The facts of weather raised
To a mystery

White on the world he knew
And all he owned.
Snow? Here? he mused. I see.
High time I learned.

Now that the boys have got
the farm in hand,
With all they know, and claim
To understand.

Here, guessing what he meant
Had much to do
With that black earth dread old men
Are given to,

He stooped to break the sheer
Crust with delight
At finding the cold unknown
So deeply bright,

At feeling it take his prints
So softly deep,
As if it thought he knew
Enough to sleep,

Or else so little he
Might seek to shift
Its weight of wintry light
By a single drift,

Perceiving which, he scuffed
His slippered feet
And scooped a handful up
To taste, and eat

In memory of the fact
That even he
Might not have seen the end
Of reality. . . .

Then, turning, he tiptoed in
To a bedroom, smiled,
And wakened a murmuring child
And another child.

OUT AFTER DARK

Geoffrey Lehmann

I'm only sorry I've no child to show him.
Out driving after dusk my headlights fumble
Through dust and trees, undulate over tarred
    roads.
My father somewhere in the night is plodding
Dark hills he cannot understand, loose earth,
My father innocent, frail as rice paper,
Mild at the end, not knowing he has cancer,
But knowing that he's finished, gentle, silent,
So selling bit by bit his watches, silver,
The crumbling mansion with its vast verandas,
Its palms and cedar doors with cut glass handles
Hiving the light in honey-coloured facets,
House where we never lived, our lives unlived.
My headlights brush moths, scrub, and scan and
    wander,
But what I'm looking for is past not present,
A hot night twenty years ago, myself
A child reading "The Moonstone", all of us
    waiting
In canvas chairs for trains eternally late,
Bells ringing as we lumber luggage aboard,
Pineapple fields lit by our passing carriage.
Reflected in the glass, our figures seated
Beneath a lamp travel dark fields and rivers.
Loving, transitory, we never existed.

FIVE DAYS LATE

Geoffrey Lehmann

Late, five days late. At night in sleep they fumble
To feel the cool gold ring which is not there,
The space beside them which is sometimes man,
The single girls who laughed and ran from
    Daddy.
The wind-chimes stir. From their high rented
    rooms
The city is a wave of black stars breaking
In violet abysses, clouds of gasoline.
Pads of rouge, scent bottles, eyelash brushes
Are mummified in the dressing table mirror.
They travel nightmare elevators up
And down with flimsy shift fanned by ozone,
In an empty building, buttons pressed by no one.
Memories of kisses hang around their necks
Like stones, dolls fall from burning aeroplanes,
And ghosts of children crawl in moonlit playpens,
Clamber and strain for milk from dormant breasts,
Breasts which have never existed, dangling play-
    things
Craving the press of life, the tug of lips,
Anguished wombs twisting, curving to be filled
With Baby and his big blind head of bread,
The bawling nightmare spilling porridge on floors,
The handful of tears blowing a paper trumpet,
The bib daubed with chocolate kissing the stars
    goodbye.
In rented rooms the coffee cups are cold,
And single girls toss in their night of doubt.
When morning wakes with blood, they weep, are
    safe.

THE TELESCOPE AT SIDING SPRING

Geoffrey Lehmann

The Warrumbungles loomed like derelict whales.
All night the whispering bush, dark, empty land-
    scape,
Great mountains under shoals of browsing stars
Condensed your thoughts as lonely country does.
In woollen earmuffs, jackets firmly zipped
You moved in windless cold, boots sharp on
    concrete,
And the great mirror slowly turning followed
And drank a scratch of light your eyes were
    blind to.
Patiently magnified for hours through mirrors
A star chiselled a message on dark film,
A tentative diamond flickered in frail water.

Date Due